Pete the Cat

The Petes Go Marching

by James Dean

HARPER

An Imprint of HarperCollinsPublishers

The artist used pen and ink with watercolor and acrylic paint on
300lb hot press paper to create the illustrations for this book.
Typography by Jeanne L. Hogle
17 18 19 20 21 SCP 10 9 8 7 6 5 4 3 2 1

First Edition

The Petes go marching one by one, hurrah, hurrah!
The Petes go marching one by one, hurrah, hurrah!

The Petes go marching one by one.
The groovy one stops to have some fun.
And they all go marching down to town
to get out of the rain,

BOOM! BOOM! BOOM!

The Petes go marching two by two, hurrah, hurrah!
The Petes go marching two by two, hurrah, hurrah!

The Petes go marching two by two.
The groovy one stops to meet the crew.
And they all go marching down to town
to get out of the rain, BOOM!
BOOM!
BOOM!

The Petes go marching three by three, hurrah, hurrah!
The Petes go marching three by three, hurrah, hurrah!

The Petes go marching three by three.
The groovy one stops for a tambourine.
And they all go marching down to town
to get out of the rain, BOOM! BOOM! BOOM!

The Petes go marching four by four, hurrah, hurrah!
The Petes go marching four by four, hurrah, hurrah!

The Petes go marching four by four.
The groovy one stops by at the store.
And they all go marching down to town
to get out of the rain, BOOM! BOOM! BOOM!

The Petes go marching five by five, hurrah, hurrah!
The Petes go marching five by five, hurrah, hurrah!

The Petes go marching five by five.
The groovy one stops to take a drive.
And they all go marching down to town
to get out of the rain, BOOM! BOOM! BOOM!

The Petes go marching six by six, hurrah, hurrah!
The Petes go marching six by six, hurrah, hurrah!

The Petes go marching six by six.
The groovy one stops to pick up sticks.
And they all go marching down to town
to get out of the rain, BOOM! BOOM! BOOM!

The Petes go marching seven by seven, hurrah, hurrah!
The Petes go marching seven by seven, hurrah, hurrah!

The Petes go marching seven by seven.
The groovy one stops to play "Rock and Roll Heaven."

And they all go marching down to town
to get out of the rain,

BOOM! BOOM! BOOM!

The Petes go marching eight by eight, hurrah, hurrah!
The Petes go marching eight by eight, hurrah, hurrah!

The Petes go marching eight by eight.
The groovy one stops for his bandmates.

PETE the CAT
and HIS BAND

CONCERT
TONIGHT
7 PM

And they all go marching
down to town
to get out of the rain,

BOOM! BOOM!
BOOM!

The Petes go marching nine by nine, hurrah, hurrah!
The Petes go marching nine by nine, hurrah, hurrah!

The Petes go marching nine by nine.
The groovy one stops to check the time.

And they all go marching down to town
to get out of the rain, BOOM! BOOM! BOOM!

The Petes go marching ten by ten, hurrah, hurrah!
The Petes go marching ten by ten, hurrah, hurrah!
The Petes go marching ten by ten.

The groovy one stops to shout
"THE END!"

And they all cheer for Pete the Cat
to rock out in the rain.